Where Are We?

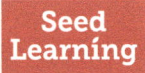
Seed Learning

car

taxi

bus

truck

train

boat

airplane

spaceship

Where are we?

We are in a taxi.

Where are we?

We are on a bus.

Where are we?

We are on a truck.

Where are we?

We are on a train.

Where are we?

We are on
an airplane.

Where are we?

We are on
a spaceship.

Let's learn about Vietnam.

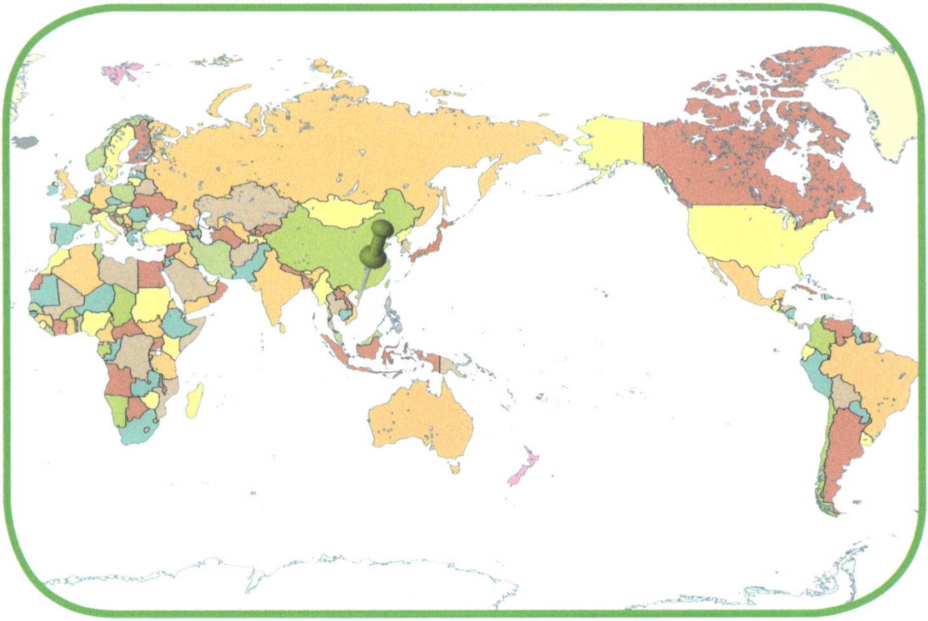

Flag of Vietnam

Ao dai